P9-DWZ-279

Zoey Serrano's
Library book!

A SURFEIT
OF SIMILES

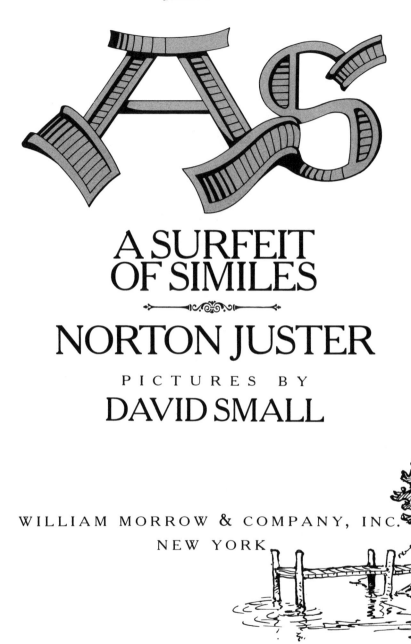

A SURFEIT
OF SIMILES

NORTON JUSTER

PICTURES BY
DAVID SMALL

WILLIAM MORROW & COMPANY, INC.
NEW YORK

Text copyright © 1989 by Norton Juster
Illustrations copyright © 1989 by David Small
Inquiries should be addressed to
William Morrow and Company, Inc.,
105 Madison Avenue,
New York, NY 10016.

Printed in the United States of America.
1 2 3 4 5 6 7 8 9 10

Library of Congress Cataloging-in-Publication Data

Juster, Norton.
As : a surfeit of similes / by Norton Juster :
pictures by David Small.
p.   cm.
Summary: Defines the mode of comparison known as simile and
provides many examples in rhyming text.
ISBN 0-688-08139-8.   ISBN 0-688-08140-1 (lib. bdg.)
1. Simile—Juvenile literature.   2. English language—Comparison—
Juvenile literature.   3. English language—Terms and phrases—
Juvenile literature.   [1. Simile.   2. English language—Terms and
phrases.]   I. Small, David,   ill.   II. Title.   III. Title:
Surfeit of Similes.
PE1445.S5J8 1989
808—dc19   88-8449   CIP   AC

For Allison and Eric,
as shiny as pearls

"What's a simile?"

"Isn't it one of those spicy sausages you put on a sandwich?"

"That's a salami."

"I thought Salami was that lady who cut off John the Baptist's head. They say that when she danced, she was as graceful as a willow."

"That was Salome, and I think that's a simile."
"It is? Can we do that again?"

As poor as a church mouse
As thin as a rail

As smooth as a porpoise
As rough as a gale

As brave as a lion
As spry as a cat
As bright as a penny
As weak as a rat

As proud as a peacock
As sly as a fox

As mad as a hatter
As strong as an ox

As fair as a lily
As empty as air
As fresh as a daisy
As cross as a bear

As round as an apple
As hot as the mustard
As cunning as snakes
As creamy as custard

As firm as a melon
As brown as a berry
As fresh as a peach
As black as a cherry

As pure as an angel
As clever as zippers
As awkward as crutches
As friendly as slippers

As hard as a rock
As white as a sheet
As sweet as a lute
As red as a beet

As light as a feather
As wrinkled as prunes
As stiff as a poker
Elusive as tunes

As creepy as spiders
As harsh as a snub
As cheerful as bluebirds
As warm as a tub

As moist as the dew
As quiet as pride
Uncertain as weather
As sure as the tide

As sharp as a stick
As due as the rent
As foul as a sty

"Do you get the intent?"

"Of course you have to be careful what you compare things to."

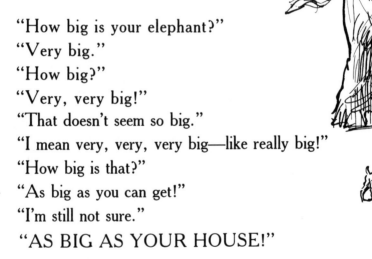

"How big is your elephant?"
"Very big."
"How big?"
"Very, very big!"
"That doesn't seem so big."
"I mean very, very, very big—like really big!"
"How big is that?"
"As big as you can get!"
"I'm still not sure."

"AS BIG AS YOUR HOUSE!"

"Thanks, but I live in a very small house. Would you like to try again?"

As flat as a pancake

As warm as your socks

As dead as a doornail

As constant as clocks

As patient as lizards
As heavy as lead
As slow as the ketchup
As safe as your bed

As serious as checkers
As cozy as kittens
As short as bad tempers
As lost as your mittens

As still as a statue
As busy as bees
As scary as heights
As silly as knees

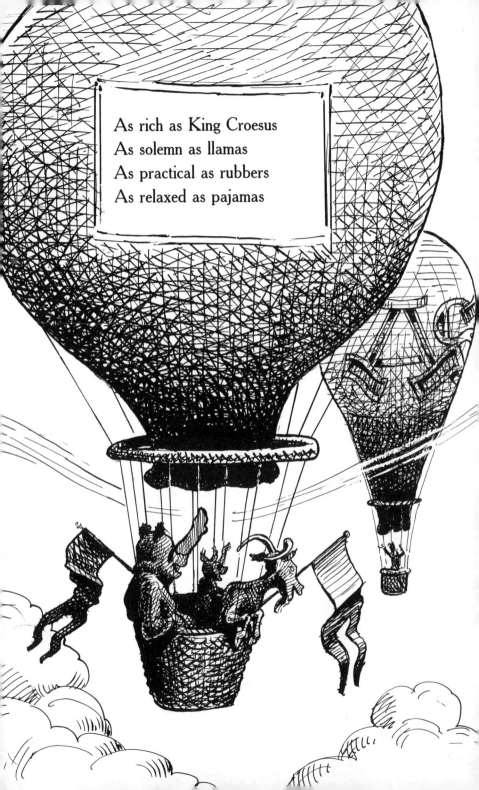

As rich as King Croesus
As solemn as llamas
As practical as rubbers
As relaxed as pajamas

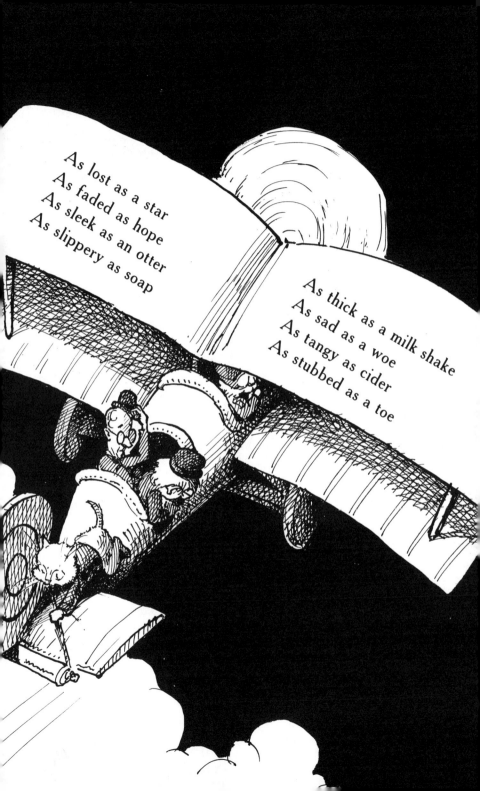

As salty as kippers
As bright as the morning
As fit as a fiddle
As cool as an awning

As proud as a parent
As plump as corn fritters
As blunt as the truth
As dull as no-hitters

*"Sometimes, what something isn't—can tell you
a lot about what it is. . . ."*

As comfortable as a hairbrush in bed
As graceful as a hippopotamus on roller skates
As clean as a coal miner's fingernails

As convenient as an unabridged dictionary
As reassuring as a dentist's smile
As exciting as a plateful of cabbage

As pleasant as ice water in your shoe
As welcome as a rainy Saturday
As easy as collecting feathers in a hurricane

"Gee, thanks. That's as interesting as the
magazines in a doctor's waiting room. Do you have
any more?"

As fierce as a leopard

As drunk as a sailor

As noisy as starlings
As grim as a jailer

As soft as a sofa
As drowsy as puppies

As prickly as thistles
As sick as a dog

As tight as a suture
As fat as a hog

As spicy as gossip
Alike as green peas

As mysterious as stew
As smelly as cheese

As brittle as crackers
As deaf as a post
As twisted as pretzels
As crisp as the toast

As boring as uncles
As grave as morticians
As dreadful as funerals
As strong as traditions

As dismal as bowling
As black as a slate
As tedious as sermons
As useless as hate

As helpful as boy scouts
As long as a train
As cruel as a hoax
As clogged as a drain

As faint as a whisper
As certain as Christmas
Contagious as yawning
As slim as an isthmus

"But you can overdo it."
"I can't see a thing!"
"It's as dark as a vampire's shadow."
"As dark as an undiscovered cave."
"As dark as the back of a beetle."
"As dark as a dreadful superstition."
"As dark as midnight at the bottom of a well."
"As dark as a miser's pocketbook."
"As dark as the woods when you're lost."
"As dark as a terrible secret."
"That's funny, I just can't see it.
It must be too dark. Let's just keep going."
AS

As blind as a bat

As queer as a duck

As different as noses
As fickle as luck

As still as a corpse
As sharp as a sleuth

As old as some jokes
As far as Duluth

As wise as an owl
As sure as prediction

As useless as warts
As true as good fiction

As smart as a whip
As neat as a pin

As dear as a dolly
As ugly as sin

As stubborn as laces
As grim as a drought
As rude as the garlic
As sauer as kraut

As kind as grandparents
As persistent as creditors
As gnawing as doubt
As picky as editors

As varied as snowflakes
As handy as tacks
As thrilling as danger
Unlikely as yaks

As expected as presents
As deep as true love
As uncertain as graduates
As snug as your glove

As lively as polkas
As contrary as kites
As meager as praise
As precious as rights

As tempting as elsewhere
As delicate as lace
As full as a tick
As fast as a chase

As vague as a longing
As destructive as time
As angry as hornets
As relentless as rhyme

As brittle as glass
As tight as a screw
As gentle as caring
And as sad as "Adieu"

"You see, it's really quite simple. A simile is just a mode of comparison employing *as* and *like* to reveal the hidden character or essence of whatever we want to describe, and through the use of fancy, association, contrast, extension, or imagination, to enlarge our understanding or perception of human experience and observation."

"Of course! It's as clear as a bell! Now, what's a surfeit?"